A

RO

THE
DICE

WILL

NEV

/ER

ABO

LISH

HANE

MALL

ARMÉ

TRANSLATED BY ROBERT BONONNO

AND JEFF CLARK

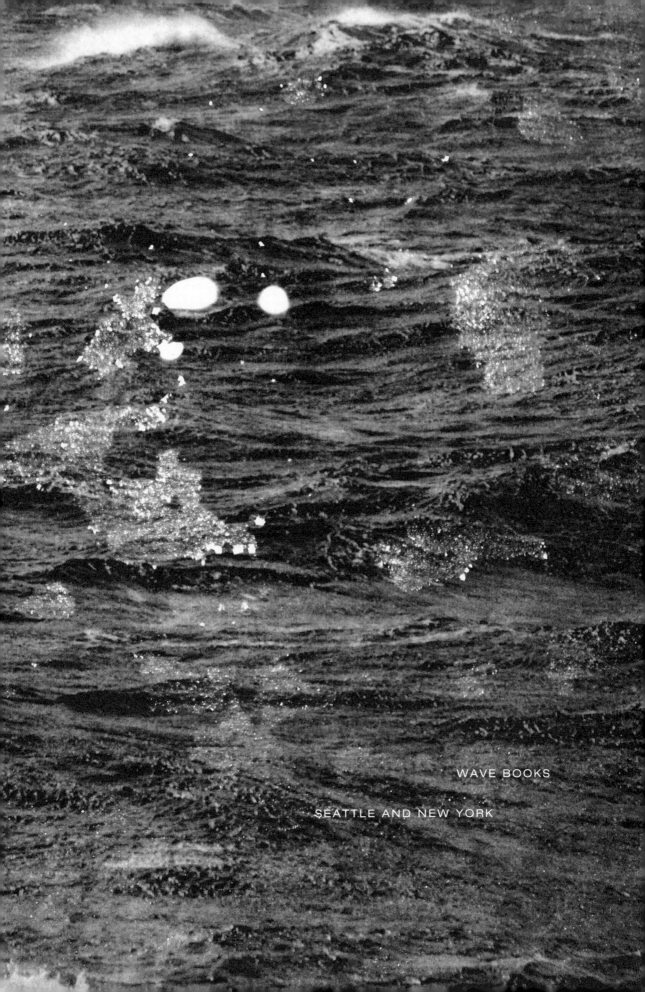

WAVE BOOKS

SEATTLE AND NEW YORK

PUBLISHED BY WAVE BOOKS

WWW.WAVEPOETRY.COM

TRANSLATION COPYRIGHT © 2015

BY ROBERT BONONNO AND JEFF CLARK

FIRST PAPERBACK EDITION, 2024

WAVE BOOKS TITLES ARE DISTRIBUTED TO THE TRADE BY

CONSORTIUM BOOK SALES AND DISTRIBUTION

PHONE: 800-283-3572 / SAN 631-760X

LIBRARY OF CONGRESS CATALOGING-IN-PUBLICATION DATA

MALLARMÉ, STÉPHANE, 1842–1898.

A ROLL OF THE DICE / STÉPHANE MALLARMÉ ; TRANSLATED FROM THE

FRENCH BY ROBERT BONONNO AND JEFF CLARK. — FIRST EDITION.

PAGES CM

ISBN 978-1-940696-04-1

I. BONONNO, ROBERT, TRANSLATOR. II. CLARK, JEFF, 1971– TRANSLATOR.

III. MALLARMÉ, STÉPHANE, 1842–1898. COUP DE DÉS JAMAIS N'ABOLIRA

LE HASARD. IV. MALLARMÉ, STÉPHANE, 1842–1898. COUP DE DÉS JAMAIS

N'ABOLIRA LE HASARD. ENGLISH. V. TITLE.

PQ2344.C6E5 2015

841'.8—DC23

2014031746

PAPERBACK ISBN: 978-1-950268-94-8

DESIGNED BY CRISIS

PRINTED IN CANADA

9 8 7 6 5 4 3 2 1

A ROLL OF THE DICE

WILL NEVER

EVEN WHEN THROWN UNDER ETERNAL

CIRCUMSTANCES

FROM THE DEPTHS OF A SHIPWRECK

THOUGH

        the Abyss

    whitened
      spreads
        furious
          beneath the flat tilt
            despairingly

              of a wing

              its own
                fallen

              beyond ancient calculations
          where the maneuver forgotten with age

                      of old he would grab hold of the helm

at his feet
          of the unanimous horizon

prepares itself
      is shaken and mixes
            in the fist that would grasp it
a fate and the winds

to be an other

                  Spirit
                      to toss it
                          into the storm
                          reopen the seam and pass proudly

detached from the secret it holds

breaks over the captain
flows through the submissive beard

straight from the man

            with no vessel
                      any
                          where futile

ancestrally not to open the clenched
                                    hand
                    beyond the useless head

            legacy in disappearance

                            to someone
                                        ambiguous

                        the future immemorial demon

having
            from voided lands
                            induced
the old man toward this supreme conjunction with probability

                        the one who
                                        his callow shadow
caressed and polished and worn and washed
                        softened by the wave and freed
            from the hard bones lost among the planks

                                    born
                                        of a dalliance
the sea by the enticing forefather or the forefather against the sea
            idle fortune

                                                        Betrothal
whose
            veil of illusion reflected their fear
            as the ghost with a gesture

                        will falter
                        will collapse

                            madness

ABOLISH

AS IF

A simple

in silence

in some nearby

flutters

insinuation

wrapped in irony

                  or

                    mystery

                              hurled

                                    howled

whirlwind of hilarity and horror

above the abyss

                          without scattering it

                                        or fleeing

                        and so soothes the virgin sign

                                                            AS IF

lost solitary feather

unless

a midnight toque meets or grazes it
        and immobilizes
            upon the velvet crushed by a dark burst of laughter

            this rigid whiteness

derisive
                    against the sky
        too much
                not to mark
                    tightly
                        one who is

            bitter prince of the reef

                    heroically coiffed
        irresistible but contained
            by his small virile mind
                        in lightning

anxious

        expiatory and pubescent

                  silent

                The lucid and lordly crest

                 on the invisible brow

              glitters

                 then shades

               a sweet tenebrous stature

                  in its siren torsion

                 with last impatient scales

laughter

that

IF

of vertigo

upright

long enough
to slap
forked

a rock

false manor
all at once
dissolved in mist

which imposed
a limit on infinity

IT WAS

stellar issue

IT WOULD BE

worse

neither

more nor less

indifferently but as much

THE NUMBER

IF IT EXISTED

other than as a scattered hallucination of agony

IF IT BEGAN AND IF IT CEASED

welling up though denied and confined when visible

at last

by some profusion spilled in scarcity

IF IT CALCULATED

evidence of the sum however small

IF IT ILLUMINATED

CHANCE

Falls

the feather

rhythmic suspense of the sinister

to bury itself

in natal foam

where its delirium once leapt to a summit

bleached

by the identical neutrality of the abyss

NOTHING

of the memorable crisis
or if it were
the event

fulfilled in light of all voided outcomes

                    human

        WILL HAVE TAKEN PLACE
      an ordinary elevation pours absence

                            BUT THE PLACE
some inferior splashing as if to disperse the empty act
           abruptly which otherwise
                by its lie
         would have justified
             the loss

in these regions
          of the uncertainty
                    in which all reality is dissolved

EXCEPT

at the altitude

PERHAPS

so distant that a place

merges with the beyond

        beyond the interest

     shown to it

       in general

by some obliquity by such declivity

        of fires

   toward

    these must be

    the Seven Stars the North as well

        A CONSTELLATION

    cold because forgotten and disused

      not to the extent

      that it fails to enumerate

     on some vacant and superior surface

      the successive shock

        starlike

    of a complete accounting still unformed

watchful

    doubtful

      rolling

       brilliant and contemplative

        before stopping

      at some final place of consecration

      All Thought is a Roll of the Dice

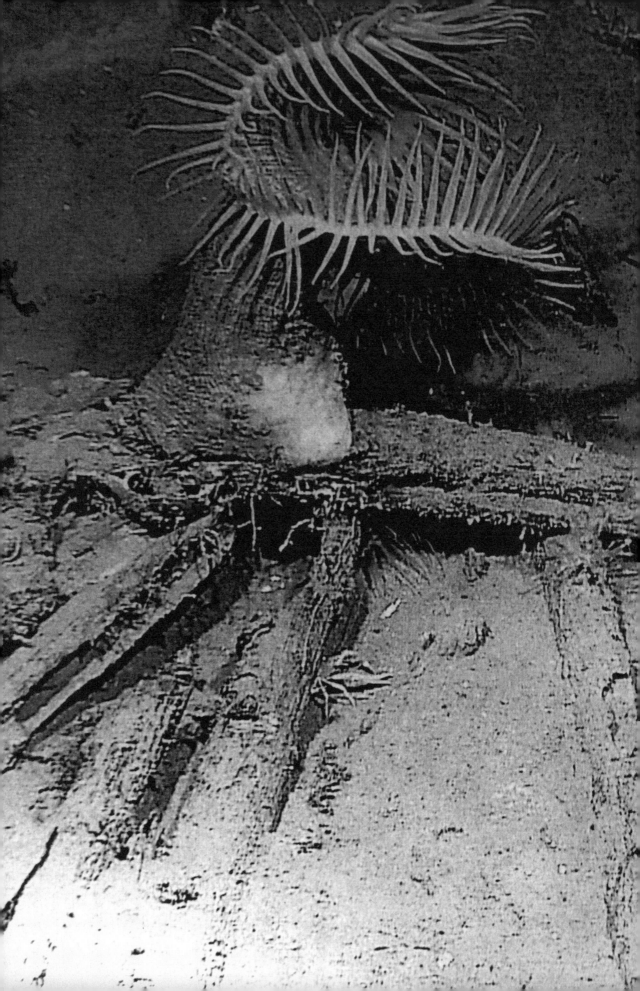

UN COUP DE DÉS

simple

enroulée avec ironie
                    ou
                            le mystère
                                        précipité
                                                    hurlé

tourbillon d'hilarité et d'horreur

autour du gouffre
                        sans le joncher
                                    ni fuir

                    et en berce le vierge indice

                                        COMME SI

plume solitaire éperdue

sauf

que la rencontre ou l'effleure une toque de minuit
et immobilise
au velours chiffonné par un esclaffement sombre

cette blancheur rigide

dérisoire
en opposition au ciel
trop
pour ne pas marquer
exigüment
quiconque

prince amer de l'écueil

s'en coiffe comme de l'héroïque
irrésistible mais contenu
par sa petite raison virile
en foudre

soucieux

      expiatoire et pubère

                        muet

La lucide et seigneuriale aigrette
au front invisible
scintille
puis ombrage
une stature mignonne ténébreuse
en sa torsion de sirène

par d'impatientes squames ultimes

rire

que

SI

de vertige

debout

le temps
de souffleter
bifurquées

un roc

faux manoir
tout de suite
évaporé en brumes

qui imposa
une borne à l'infini

C'ÉTAIT

issu stellaire

CE SERAIT

pire

non

davantage ni moins

indifféremment mais autant

LE NOMBRE

EXISTÂT-IL

autrement qu'hallucination éparse d'agonie

COMMENÇÂT-IL ET CESSÂT-IL

sourdant que nié et clos quand apparu

enfin

par quelque profusion répandue en rareté

SE CHIFFRÂT-IL

évidence de la somme pour peu qu'une

ILLUMINÂT-IL

LE HASARD

Choit

    la plume

        rythmique suspens du sinistre

                s'ensevelir

        aux écumes originelles

naguères d'où sursauta son délire jusqu'à une cime

            flétrie

        par la neutralité identique du gouffre

RIEN

de la mémorable crise
ou se fût
l'évènement

accompli en vue de tout résultat nul

                humain

       N'AURA EU LIEU

      une élévation ordinaire verse l'absence

                  QUE LE LIEU

inférieur clapotis quelconque comme pour disperser l'acte vide

            abruptement qui sinon

          par son mensonge

            eût fondé

           la perdition

dans ces parages

         du vague

            en quoi toute réalité se dissout

EXCEPTÉ

à l'altitude

PEUT-ÊTRE

aussi loin qu'un endroit

fusionne avec au delà

                       hors l'intérêt
                 quant à lui signalé
                               en général
selon telle obliquité par telle déclivité
                               de feux

        vers
              ce doit être
                   le Septentrion aussi Nord

                          UNE CONSTELLATION

                 froide d'oubli et de désuétude
                          pas tant
                       qu'elle n'énumère
                sur quelque surface vacante et supérieure
                    le heurt successif
                            sidéralement
                 d'un compte total en formation

veillant
            doutant
                  roulant
                      brillant et méditant

                              avant de s'arrêter
                  à quelque point dernier qui le sacre

                  Toute Pensée émet un Coup de Dés

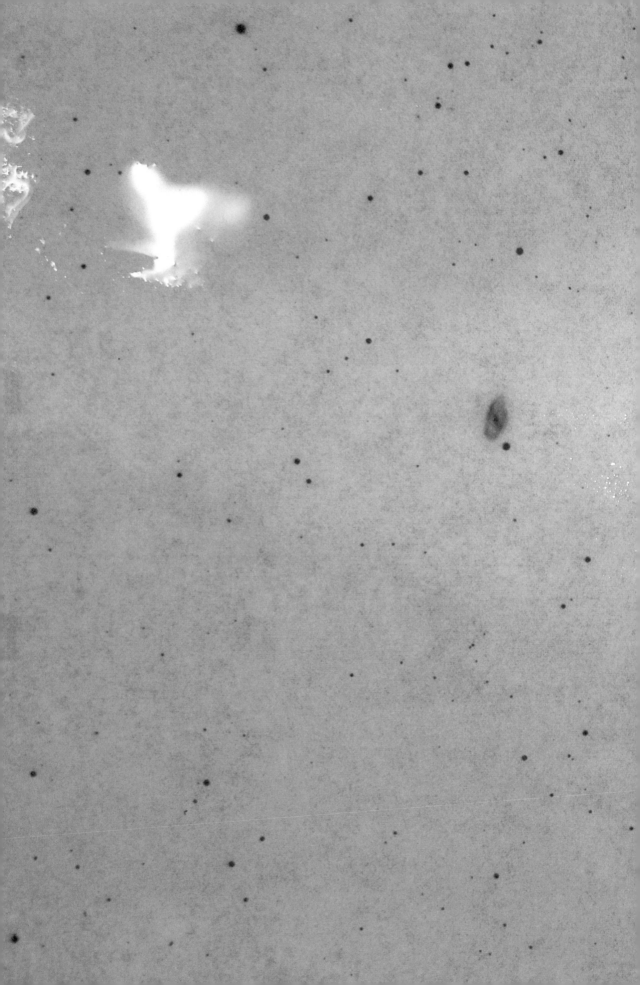

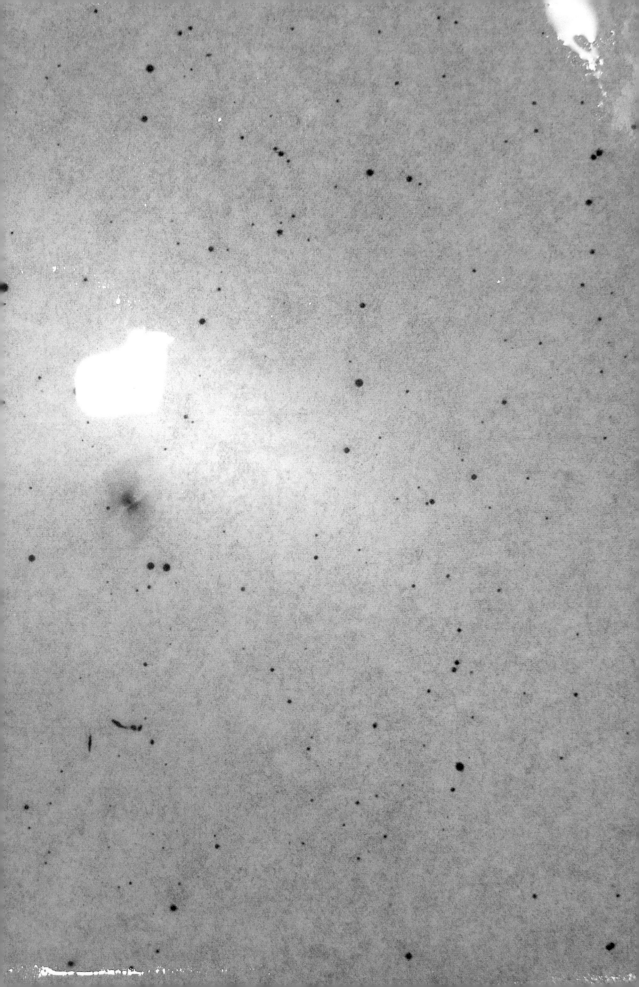

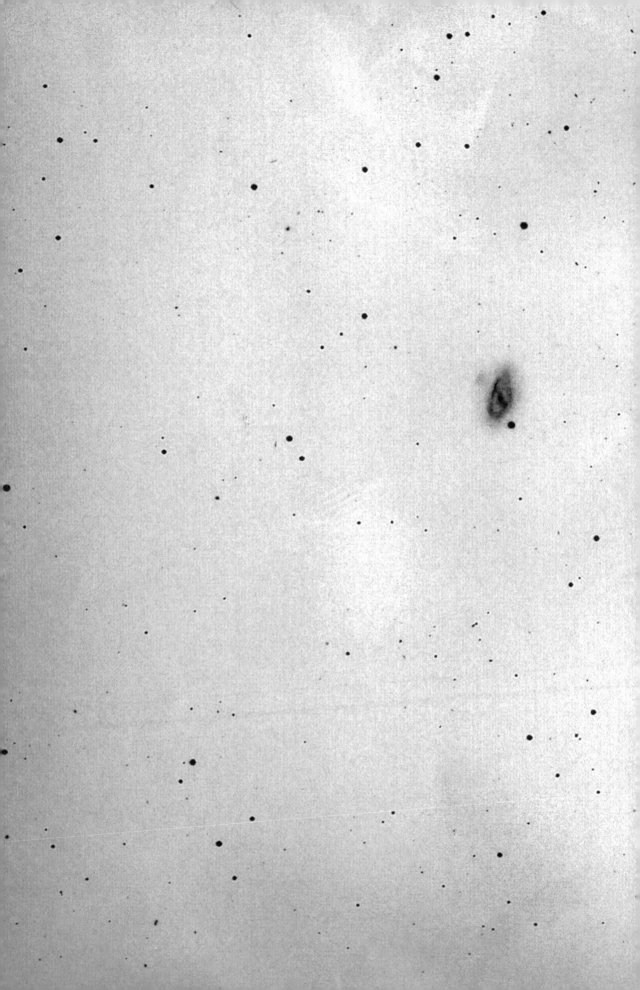

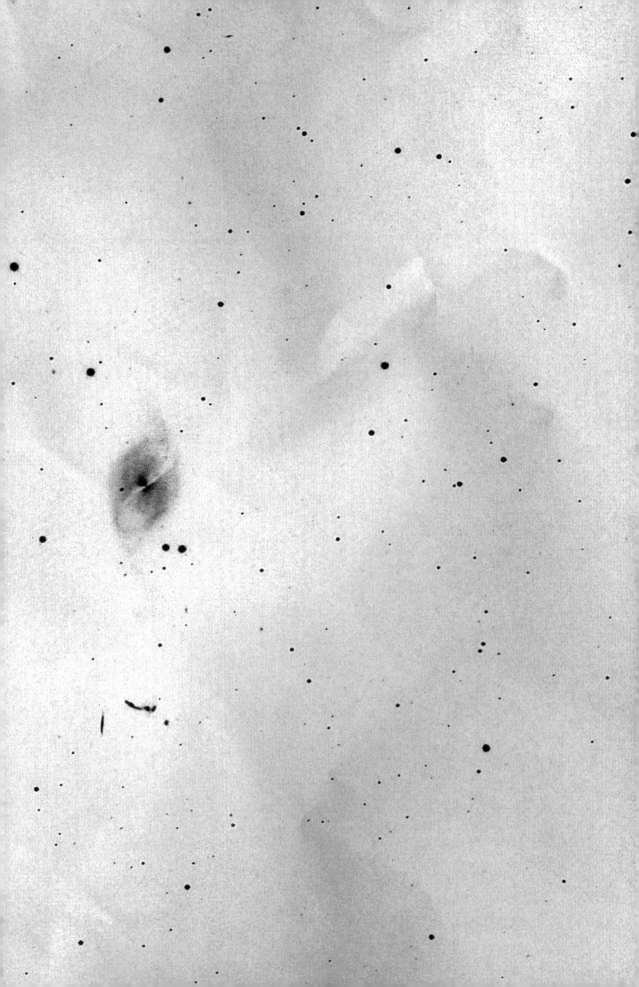